Little
DINOSAUR

Martin Waddell

Illustrated by Tim Archbold

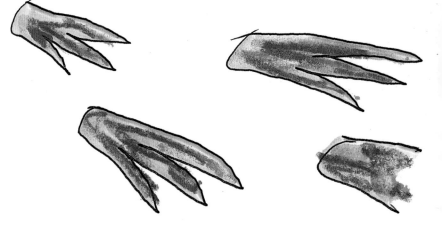

OXFORD
UNIVERSITY PRESS

1

The Treasure Hunt

Sam lived next door to Emma. They were best friends, so they always did things together.

One day, Emma went down to
Pirate Cove, and she started to dig in
the sand.

'What are you digging for, Emma?'
asked Sam.

'I'm digging for treasure,' said
Emma. 'This is Pirate Cove, so there
should be treasure buried somewhere.'

Sam climbed down into the hole to help Emma dig, and then...

CLANG!

Emma's spade hit something hard under the sand.

5

They dug up the thing that had clanged and pulled it out of the hole with a rope.

They stood and looked at the thing. It was bright green with brown shiny bits.

'It's a huge cannonball!' Emma
decided. 'Someone fired it at a pirate
and missed!'

The sun shone on the huge
cannonball for the first time in years.
The huge cannonball *twitched*, as
though something inside it had
wakened and stretched, and started
to grow.

It was a very small twitch, so Sam
and Emma both missed it.

'First thing tomorrow, we'll take it to
school!' Sam and Emma decided.

The next day, Sam and Emma marched into school.

Emma was wheeling the old wheelbarrow and Sam was helping her push.

There was something big in the wheelbarrow, hidden under Sam's dad's old coat.

'What's this, Emma dear?' asked the
Head, keeping well away from the
wheelbarrow.

'Look!' Emma said proudly, and she
whipped the coat off.

'It's a huge cannonball and we found it!' said Sam. 'We're giving it to the school!'

Everyone cheered them for giving a huge cannonball to their school.

Sam and Emma were famous.

The newspaper called them THE CANNONBALL KIDS.

THE CANNONBALL KIDS

Two local children have found an old cannonball on the beach...

Everyone was very pleased.

2

That Night

That night, the moon shone on the big cannonball.

It moved, just a bit. No one was there, so no one saw it move.

Then it started to grow, slowly at first, and then faster and faster.

It grew and it grew and it grew...

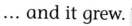 ... and it grew.

Then it twitched, and it stopped...

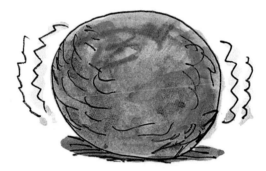

... as though something inside it had been growing too fast, and needed to rest.

Then it grew a bit more...

... and it **BURST!**

There was a cloud of green
smoke and out of the smoke
stepped a baby dinosaur.

3

'We're In This Together!'

'Oh, gosh!' gasped the Head the next morning, looking into the school hall.

There wasn't much left in the hall – no curtains or gym mats or tables or chairs. They'd all been chewed up by *something* with very big teeth.

There was a large hole in the wall,
where there had been a big window.

'Miss! Miss!' called Sam and Emma,
looking in through the hole in the wall.

'What is it, dears?' asked the Head.

'There's a baby dinosaur fast asleep on our football pitch!' Sam and Emma told her. 'Our cannonball must have been a lost dinosaur egg. It just *looked* like a huge cannonball.'

Everyone rushed out to look.

There, on the school football pitch, was the baby dinosaur, with its tail wrapped around the nearest goal post.

'It might eat the whole school!' Sam whispered to Emma.

'We're in this together!' said Emma.

'Send for the boss of the zoo!' cried the Head.

The boss of the zoo came with a lot
of zoo men, carrying nets. The whole
school was lined up at the end of the
pitch, safe from the small dinosaur.

'We'll save your school from this dangerous dinosaur, Madam,' the boss of the zoo told the Head. 'We'll put it in our zoo and we'll be famous forever!'

The small dinosaur opened one eye, and it blinked. Then it looked at the men and the nets, and it started to shiver.

'It's *our* dinosaur that *we* gave to the school. We're not having this!' cried Sam and Emma. 'It isn't fair! All those big men chasing one baby dinosaur!'

'But what can we do?' said the Head.

'Leave it to us!' said Sam and Emma.

'*You?*' snarled the boss of the zoo. 'How can two little kids save a whole school from a dangerous dinosaur?'

4

'Ug?'

Even a baby dinosaur is quite big,
and this one was much bigger than
Sam and Emma. It had shiny skin and
big teeth.

'It might eat us,' Emma shivered.

'It might not!' Sam said. 'It might be
a veggy.'

They walked up to the goal post. The baby dinosaur blinked, and a big tear rolled down its long nose.

'It's only a little one, Emma,' Sam whispered.

'A very B-I-G little one!' Emma whispered back. 'It's missing its mummy, I think.'

Sam was brave. He
reached up and rubbed
the baby dinosaur's nose.

Then Emma softly
tickled its ear with
the tip of one finger.

'There, there, baby,'
cooed Emma. 'Don't cry.'

'We won't let them put you in the zoo!' Sam said, stroking its head.

'Ug?' said the baby dinosaur.

'Ug!' answered Emma, drying its tears with her hanky.

'Ug!' Sam agreed, though he didn't quite know what 'Ug' meant. He just kept on stroking and hoping.

The little dinosaur looked at Sam and Emma.

It gave a little dinosaur smile, showing its very big teeth.

Then it rolled on its back, with its legs in the air.

The baby dinosaur wriggled about like a puppy, wagging its very long tail.

Everyone cheered, except the man from the zoo. He drove off in his van, looking very cross.

Now the school has its own dinosaur as a pet. It lives at the end of the football pitch.

Sam and Emma bring it old trees and grass cuttings and left-over school dinners each day, after class.

They wash it and brush it and polish its teeth. They take it for walks around the school field, and each week it grows a bit...

...BIGGER!

About the author

I knew digging up a big egg would be an interesting way to start a story. I thought a baby dinosaur chewing everything in the school hall would work, and the idea that it was a veggy dinosaur got me out of  the will-it-eat-everybody problem at the end. That was the idea-trail I followed when I planned this story.

If you had begun with digging up a big egg... what would *you* have made happen?